A BOOK OF AUTOGRAPH VERSES

Yours Till
Niagara Falls

Newly Illustrated Edition

Compiled by Lillian Morrison
Illustrated by Sylvie Wickstrom

THOMAS Y. CROWELL
NEW YORK

Yours Till Niagara Falls: A Book of Autograph Verses
Text copyright © 1950, 1990 by Lillian Morrison
Illustrations copyright © 1990 by Sylvie Kantorovitz Wickstrom

Printed in the United States of America. For information address Thomas Y. Crowell
Junior Books, 10 East 53rd Street, New York, NY 10022.
ISBN: 0-690-04876-9 (lib. bdg.)
Library of Congress Catalog Card Number: 89-82520
1 2 3 4 5 6 7 8 9 10
Newly Illustrated Edition

To
Aguilar
the place and the people

CONTENTS

Roses Are Red

Roses are red,
Violets are blue.
Sugar is sweet,
And so are you.

Roses may be red,
Violets may be blue.
But there ain't no maybe
'Bout what I think of you.

Roses are red,
Pickles are green.
My face is a holler,
But yours is a scream.

Roses are red,
Violets are blue.
God made me pretty,
But what happened to you?

3

You love yourself, you think you're grand.
You go to the movies and hold your hand.
You put your arm around your waist,
And when you get fresh you slap your face.

Marguerite, go wash your feet.
The Board of Health's across the street.

If giggles and smiles
Could keep you alive,
You would live to be
One hundred and five.

Policeman, policeman
Do your duty!
Here comes Rosie,
The American beauty!

Fair are the lilies
That float on the brook,
But fairer the girl
Who owns this book.

The rose is red
And the violet blue.
The pink is pretty
And so are you.

Fire! Fire!
False alarm.
Here comes Mazie
In a fireman's arms.

Mirror, mirror, on the wall,
Who's the smartest one of all?
Jason, Jason, he's the brain.
Mirror, mirror, you're insane.

Jersey girls are pretty,
Boston girls are smart;
But it takes a New Yorker
To win a boy's heart.

I'm not a Northern beauty,
I'm not a Southern rose.
I'm just a little schoolgirl
With freckles on my nose.

Roses are red,
They grow in this region.
If I had your face,
I'd join the Foreign Legion.

Poor little Ida,
Sitting on a fence,
Trying to make a dollar
Out of 99 cents.

Peaches grow in Florida,
California too.
But it takes a state like Iowa
To grow a peach like you.

God made the ocean,
God made the beach,
But when he made Alice,
He sure made a peach.

Satellites are red,
Rockets are blue.
If you don't behave,
I'll send you up too.

My house is situated near a pond.
Drop in sometime.

Roses are red,
Violets are blue.
When it rains,
I think of you.
Drip, drip, drip.

Calling car 1!
Calling car 2!
Gary and Paul
Just escaped from the zoo.

As the years go by
And the pounds roll off,
You'll grow up to be
A real show-off.

You drink a lot of soda,
You eat a lot of cream.
But when you get older,
You'll be someone's dream.

Johnny is a buttercup,
Johnny is a daisy.
Johnny is a bad boy
Who drives the girls all crazy.

Sugar is sweet,
Coal is black.
Do me a favor
And sit on a tack.

What! Write in Your Album!

What! Write in your book!
Where gentlemen look!
Not I!
I am shy!
Good-bye!

Round went the album;
Hither it came
For me to write,
So here's my name.

It tickles me,
It makes me laugh
To think
You want my autograph.

I am no poet.
I have no fame.
But just the same
I'll sign my name.

In this book I'll gladly sign
Right upon the dotted line.

Sally Jones

You asked me to sign your autograph,
But I'd rather have your photograph,
So let me know by telegraph
How you like my paragraph.

I thought, I thought, I thought in vain,
At last I thought I'd write my name.

Alas, alas, I am so dumb,
I cannot write in this album.

I want to write something original,
But I don't know how to begin.
There's nothing original about me
Unless it's original sin.

Sometimes I'm naughty,
Sometimes I'm nice.
Now I'll be naughty
And sign my name thrice.

Lucy Brown
Lucy Brown
Lucy Brown

(For a white page)

May you always be as pure as this page before I wrote on it.

On this page,
Pure and white,
Only a friend would dare to write.

I write on white
To be polite
And leave the yellow
For some rude fellow.

(For a pink page)
I beg you on this page of pink
Not to fall for a sailor's wink.

Forgive me, Jane, for being bold.
I was going to write my name in gold,
But since I picked this page of pink,
I'll have to write my name in ink.

(For a blue page)
I chose BLUE.
Because my friendship's true.

I hope you never feel like the color of this page.

I write upon this page of blue.
To wish success in all you do.

Some write up. Some write down. But I'll be different and write around.

What! Write in your album!
What shall it be?
Just two little words
"Remember me."

I bet you I can make any fool in town
Turn this album upside down.

I'm the toughest boy in the city,
I'm the toughest boy in the town,
I'm the boy that spoiled your book
By writing upside down.

_____

_____

Some blank verse from a blank mind.

_____

_____

_____

_____

Four lines from a lazy poet.

Look Who's Graduating

Open the gate!
Open the gate!
Here comes Lily
The graduate!

Birds on the mountain,
Fish in the sea.
How you ever graduated
Is a mystery to me.

Friends, Romans, countrymen,
Lend me your ears.
Look who's graduating
After all these years.

Remember Miss Rankin,
Tall and lanky.
Remember Miss Clay,
Short and cranky.
Remember Miss Lichtman,
Fair and square.
Remember Mr. Alber,
Without any hair.

An eagle flew from North to South
With little Mary in his mouth.
When he saw she was no fool,
He dropped her off at high school.

I wasn't Bored of Education till I met you.

Don't you worry,
Don't you fret;
We can't all be
Teacher's pet.

God made the bees;
The bees made honey.
We do the work
And teacher gets the money.

Teachers are religious souls;
They go to church on Sunday
To pray to God to give them strength
To worry us kids on Monday.

United States is your nation,
Fordham is your station,
But it took Our Lady Queen of Help
To give you an education.

First we meet,
Then we part.
That's the sorrow
Of a graduate's heart.

Latin is a dead language,
It's plain enough to see.
It killed off all the Romans,
And now it's killing me.

In days of old
When knights were bold
And teachers weren't invented,
You'd go to school
And be a fool
And come out at 3:00 contented.

In years to come
I'll recall memories sweet
Of the pitter-patter down the hall
Of your big feet.

Remember the beer,
Remember the ale.
Remember the days
We spent in jail.

Remember A,
Remember B.
Remember the day
We both got D.

Remember the fork,
Remember the spoon.
Remember the fun
In Sullivan's room.

*True Friends
Are Like Diamonds*

True friends are like diamonds,
Precious but rare;
False friends are like autumn leaves,
Scattered everywhere.

Friends are like melons.
Shall I tell you why?
To find a good one
You must one hundred try.

Remember well and bear in mind
That a faithful friend is hard to find.
And when you find one that is true,
Change not the old one for the new.

If I were a head of lettuce,
I'd cut myself in two.
I'd give the leaves to all my friends
And save the heart for you.

When twilight drops her curtain
And pins it with a star,
Remember I'm your true friend
No matter where you are.

A ring is round and has no end. So is my love for you, my friend.

There are golden ships,
There are silver ships,
But the best ship
Is "Friendship."

In the golden chain of friendship, consider me a link.

May the hinges of our friendship never rust.

Love your friends, love them well,
But to your friends no secrets tell;
For if your friend becomes your foe
Your secrets everyone will know.

Tell me quick
Before I faint,
Is we friends
Or is we ain't?

49

If you get to Heaven
Before I do,
Bore a little hole
And pull me through.

If in Heaven
We don't meet,
Hand in hand
We'll stand the heat.
And if it gets intensely hot,
Pepsi-Cola hits the spot.

In the chimney of your future, please count me as a brick.

When you are sick
And going to die,
Call me up
And I will cry.

Choose not your friends
From outward show.
Feathers float,
But pearls lie low.

In the breadbox of your affections, regard me as a crumb.

I like coffee, I like tea.
I like you and you like me.

Not like the rose shall our friendship wither,
But like the evergreen live forever.

Until two nickels don't make a dime,
Consider yourself a friend of mine.

I met you as a stranger,
I leave you as a friend.
I hope we meet in Heaven,
Where friendship never ends.

Yours till butter flies.

Yours till cigars box.

Yours till meatballs bounce.

Yours till the Confederates wear Union suits.

Yours till Hell freezes over and all the little devils
go ice skating.

Yours till ginger snaps.

Yours till the Statue of Liberty sits down.

Yours till the United States drinks Canada Dry.

Yours till the barn dances and the fire escapes.

Yours till the radio waves.

Yours till soda pops.

Yours till the cat fishes.

Yours till Russia cooks Turkey in Greece and
serves it on China to the Hungary U.S.A.

Yours till Dracula stops being a pain in the neck.

Yours till the mountain peeks and sees the salad dressing.

Yours till the bed spreads.

Yours till Bear Mountain gets cubs.

Yours till caterpillars wear roller skates.

Yours till Cats kill Mountains.

Yours till the kitchen sinks.

Yours till the board walks.

Yours till the oak tree develops square roots.

Yours till they feed the corn on your toes
to the calves on your legs.

Yours till Niagara Falls.

Listen, My Friend

Listen, my friend, before we part:
Never depend on a young man's heart.
A young man's heart is like a flower;
It will wither and wilt within the hour.

Ashes to ashes,
Dust to dust.
There is no man a woman can trust.
So have no man and have no sorrow,
For he's here today and gone tomorrow.

Be	good as a Christian,
Wise	as a saint;
And	when a boy asks you to
Kiss	him, tell
Him	you can't.

Beware of boys with eyes of brown;
They kiss you once and turn you down.
Beware of boys with eyes of blue;
They kiss you once and ask for two.
Beware of boys with eyes of gray;
They kiss you once and turn away.
Beware of boys with eyes of black;
They kiss you once and never come back.
You will know all kinds of joys
If only you'll beware of boys.

The sheep like the valley,
The cows like the hill,
The boys like the girls,
And I guess they always will.

Your heart is not a plaything,
Your heart is not a toy.
But if you want it broken,
Just give it to a boy.

Bless the man that takes your hand
And to the altar leads you.
But woe to the man that takes your hand
And then forgets to feed you.

Boys are like a box of snuff.
Get one whiff and that's enough.

Girls are like a nugget of gold,
Hard to get and hard to hold.

A woman's place is everyplace.

He is a fool who thinks by force or skill
To turn the current of a woman's will.

'Twas in a restaurant they first met,
Romeo and Juliet.
'Twas there that he got into debt
'Cause Rom-e-owed what Juli-et.

May God above send down a dove
With wings as sharp as a razor
To cut the heart of any man
Who loves a girl and then betrays her.

When sitting on the sofa
With your boyfriend by your side,
Beware of false kisses;
His mustache may be dyed.

Many a ship is lost at sea
For want of oil and rudder.
Many a girl has lost her guy
For flirting with another.

Some shoes are black,
Some shoes are tan.
Stop flirting with the boys
or I'll tell your old man.

If you want a taste
Of Heaven's joys,
Think more of the Lord
And less of the boys.

72

Gold is pure
And so is pearl,
But purest of all
Is an innocent girl.

BOYS
It's not in the height
It's in the heart.

You are nice to see
And good to know,
But listen, my friend,
Take it slow.

I love coffee,
I love tea.
A shoemaker's daughter
Made a heel out of me.

I Love You, I Love You

I love you, I love you
With my heart and soul.
If I had a doughnut,
I'd give you the hole.

I love you, I love you,
I love you so well,
If I had a peanut,
I'd give you the shell.

I climbed up the door
And shut the stairs.
I said my shoes
And took off my prayers.
I shut off the bed
And climbed into the light,
And all because she kissed me goodnight.

There are tulips in the garden,
There are tulips in the park.
But best of all tulips
Are the two lips that meet in the dark.

It was midnight on the back porch.
Two lips were tightly pressed.
The old man gave the signal,
And the bulldog did the rest.

You can fall from the mountains,
You can fall from above.
But the best way to fall
Is to fall in love.

My love for you
Shall never fail
As long as kitty
Has a tail.
And if that tail
Is cut in two,
That won't stop me
From loving you.

Tables are round,
Chairs are square.
You and Fred Williams
Make a good pair.

Your head is like a ball of straw;
Your nose is long and funny.
Your mouth is like a cellar door,
But still I love you, honey.

81

I wish I were a bunny
And my tail were made of fluff.
I would jump into your vanity
And be your powder puff.

I wish I were an elephant
And you were a load of hay.
I'd put you on my great big back
And carry you away.

Frankie, Frankie, don't you blush!
I caught you at the subway rush
Selling kisses 2 for 5
With Mary Johnson at your side.

May your cheeks retain their dimples,
May your heart be light and gay
Until some manly voice shall whisper,
"Sweetheart, name the day."

Little drops of dew,
Little words of love.
Am I the one to meet you
In Heaven above?

If there were a boys' camp
Across the sea,
What a great swimmer
Mary would be.

Apples on the table,
Peaches on the shelf;
If you don't love anybody,
Keep it to yourself.

When you are lonely
And in distress,
I'll send you Jack
By pony express.

(I adore you.)

My ♡ 4 u. Of

(My heart pants for you.
Of course it does.)

I love I.

I   T   A   L   Y

(I Trust And Love You)

If you love me as I love you,
No knife can cut our love in two.

Our eyes have met,
Our lips not yet,
But oh you kid,
I'll get you yet.

Roses are red,
Violets are blue.
Lend me ten dollars,
And I will love you.

Butter is butter,
Cheese is cheese.
What's a kiss
Without a squeeze?

A kiss is a germ,
Or so it's been stated.
But kiss me quick,
I'm vaccinated.

I love you once,
I love you twice.
I love you better
Than cats love mice.

Sitting by a stream,
Ellen had a dream.
She dreamed she was a little trout,
And some fine fellow fished her out.

Sure as the grass grows round the stump,
You are my darling sugar lump.

I love you, I love you,
I love you, I do.
But don't get excited,
I love monkeys too.

Two in a hammock
Ready to kiss,
When all of a sudden
It went like this!

Read see that me
up will I love
and you love you
down and you and

Pigs love pumpkins,
Cows love squash.
I love you,
I do, by gosh.

Some love ten,
Some love twenty.
But I love you,
And that is plenty.

When You Get Married

When you get married
And live upstairs,
Don't come down
And borrow my chairs.

When you get married
And live across the lake,
Send me a kiss
By the rattlesnake.

When you are married
And have 25,
Don't call it a family,
Call it a tribe.

Dear Saint Anthony,
Sweet Saint Ann,
Please give Janice
A good young man.

If ever a husband you shall have
And he these lines should see,
Tell him of your fun in school
And kiss him twice for me.

2 in a car,
little kisses,
weeks later,
Mr. and Mrs.

When Cupid shoots his arrow, I hope he Mrs. you.

Tom, Dick, or Harry,
Whom shall Rita marry?

Gloria is your name,
Single is your station.
Happy is the lucky man
Who makes the alteration.

Ducks in the millpond,
Geese in the pasture;
If you want to marry,
You'll have to talk faster.

Down by the river
Where the river flows
There stands Alice
Pretty as a rose.
There stands Robert
By her side,
Asking her to be his bride.

When you are married
And have 1, 2, 3,
Name the prettiest after me.

When you get married
And live next door,
I'll borrow your husband
To scrub my floor.

When you are married
And have a pair of twins,
Don't come to me
For safety pins.

First comes love,
Then comes marriage.
Then comes Helen
With a baby carriage.

When we are married
And living on the farm,
We will raise potatoes
As big as my arm.

When you get married
And your husband gets drunk,
Put him in a trunk
And sell him for junk.

When you get married,
Don't marry a flirt.
Marry a man
Who can buy his own shirt.

When you get married
And your husband is cross,
Pick up the broomstick
And say, "I'm the boss."

If your husband is thirsty
And wants a drink,
Take him to the kitchen
And show him the sink.

Roses are red,
Violets are blue.
When you get married,
I will too.

You're Sitting on My Head

I was sitting on a tombstone,
And a ghost came and said,
"Sorry to disturb you,
But you're sitting on my head."

Said a chambermaid to a sleeping guest,
"Get up, you lazy sinner.
We need the sheet for a tablecloth
And it's almost time for dinner."

"Your teeth are like the stars," he said,
And pressed her hand so white.
He spoke the truth, for like the stars,
Her teeth came out at night.

In jail they give you coffee,
In jail they give you tea.
In jail they give you everything
Except the doggone key.

FUNEX?
VFX.
FUNEM?
VFM.
OK, MNX.

(Have you any eggs? We have eggs.
Have you any ham? We have ham.
O.K., ham and eggs.)

Said the toe
To the sock,
"Let me through,
Let me through."
Said the sock
To the toe,
"I'll be darned
If I do."

The rooster and the chicken had a fight.
The chicken knocked the rooster out of sight.
The rooster said, "That's all right.
I'll see you in the gumbo tomorrow night."

Ginny made some doughnuts.
She made them by the peck.
One rolled out the window
And broke the horse's neck.

Anna is a silver star
Riding on a trolley car.
When the car gets off the track,
Anna wants her money back.

Oh, I've paddled on the ocean,
I've tramped on the plain.
But I never saw a window cry
Because it had a pain.

A peanut sat on the railroad track,
Its heart was all aflutter.
Along came the eight-fifteen—
Toot! Toot! Peanut butter.

Grandma has a habit
Of chewing in her sleep.
She chews on Grandpa's whiskers
And thinks it's shredded wheat.

Roses are red,
Violets are blue.
I can row a boat.
Canoe canoe?

"Go, my son, and shut the shutter."
This I heard a mother utter.
"Shutter's shut," the boy did mutter,
"I can't shut' er any shutter."

Connie, Connie in the tub.
Mother forgot to put in the plug.
Oh my Heavens! Oh my soul!
There goes Connie down the hole.

Mary had a little lamb.
Her father shot it dead.
Now Mary carries that lamb to school
Between two hunks of bread.

It's hard to lose a friend
When your heart is full of hope;
But it's worse to lose a towel
When your eyes are full of soap.

Two little boys late one night
Tried to get to Harvard on the end of a kite.
The kite string broke
And down they fell.
Instead of going to Harvard
They went to _____ .
Now don't get excited
And don't get pale.
Instead of going to Harvard,
They went to Yale.

Barbara had a cat.
It swallowed a ball of yarn.
And when the cat got kittens,
They all had sweaters on.

There was a girl from Havana
Who slipped on a peel of banana.
She wanted to swear,
But her mother was there,
So she whistled "The Star-Spangled Banner."

The fly made a visit to the grocery store,
Didn't even knock, went right in the door.
He took a bite of sugar, and he took a bite of ham,
Then sat down to rest on the grocery man.

Now I lay me down to sleep
With a bag of peanuts at my feet.
If I should die before I wake,
I'll leave it to my Uncle Jake.

By the sewer I lived;
By the sewer I died.
They said it was murder,
But it was sewercide.

Start Low, Climb High

Start low,
Climb high.
Best of luck
In senior high.

Your future lies before you
Like a shining path of snow.
Be careful how you tread,
For every step will show.

124

Success and happiness run in pairs.
If you can't find the elevator, use the stairs.

Use this ladder.

Remember the fourth commandment:
Honor thy father and mother.
Never forsake them in their old age
When you learn to love another.

Ashes to ashes,
Dust to dust.
If the Camels don't get you
The Marlboros must.

Good, better, best.
Never let it rest
Until the good is better
And the better is best.

Study and work,
Don't be a flop.
Sooner or later
You'll reach the top.

There are three things you must learn to do:

Lie   Steal   and   Drink.

Lie in the bed of success.
Steal away from bad company.
Drink from the fountain of youth.

Never B ♯
Never B ♭
Always B ♮

Look not for beauty
Nor color of skin,
But look for the heart
That is loyal within.
Beauty may fade and skin grow old,
But the heart that is loyal
Will never grow cold.

Speak good English and good English will speak for you.

A winner never quits, and a quitter never wins.

Be like a snowflake. Leave a mark but don't leave a stain.

If wisdom's ways you wisely seek,
Five things observe with care:
Of whom you speak,
To whom you speak,
And how and when and where.

Great oaks from little acorns grow.
Great aches from little toe corns grow.

Life is like a game of cards—

When you are in love it is ♥
When you are engaged it is ♦
When you are married it is ♣
When you are dead it is ♠

Be you to others kind and true
As you'd have others be to you.

Love many,
Trust few.
Always paddle your own canoe.

Though your tasks are many
And your rewards are few,
Remember that the mighty oak
Was once a nut like you.

Take the local,
Change for express.
Don't get off
Till you reach Success.

'Tis by study that we learn.
'Tis by working that we earn.
'Tis by loving that we yearn.
To whom it may concern.

Listen, my children, and you shall hear
Of the midnight ride of Sally dear.
First in a carriage, then on a wheel,
Now she rides in an automobile.

Whatever you are, be that.
Whatever you say, be true.
Straightforwardly act,
Be honest in fact,
Be nobody else but you.

Don't be ～～～～～～ (crooked)
Don't be ✕   (cross)
Just be _____ (straight)
And you'll be boss.

Count that day lost
Whose low-descending sun
Sees from your hand
No worthy action done.

When times are hard,
Write me a card.
When times get better,
Write me a letter.

When you are hungry
And have nothing to eat,
Take off your shoes
And pickle your feet.

As a rule people are fools.
When it's hot they want it cool.
When it's cool they want it hot,
Always wanting what is not.

He who knows and knows that he knows,
He is wise—follow him.
He who knows and knows not that he knows,
He is asleep—wake him.
He who knows not and knows not that he knows not,
He is a fool—shun him.
He who knows not and knows that he knows not,
He is a child—teach him.

Learn when young and not when old,
For learning is better than silver and gold.
Silver and gold will vanish away,
But a good education will never decay.

Don't wait for your ship to come in. Row out and meet it.

Always be like a piano: grand, upright, and square.

If life were a thing that money could buy,
The rich would live and the poor would die.
But God in his mercy made it so
That the rich and the poor together must go.

The past is a dream,
The present a strife;
The future a mystery,
And such is life.

Forget-Me-Not

Forget me not,
For if you do,
You'll feel the weight
Of my heavy shoe.

When you are old
And cannot see,
Put on your specs
And think of me.

When on this page
You chance to look.
Just think of me
And close the book.

146

Remember Grant,
Remember Lee.
The heck with them,
Remember me.

When you get old and your dress gets purple, remember the girl who wrote in a circle.

● Dot

Blot

Forget-me-not.

When you are in the country

standing by a hedge,

Remember it was Trixie who

wrote around the edge.

Remember the miss
Who scribbled this.

When you grow old
And have no teeth,
Remember the candy
You used to eat.

Remember me at the river,
Remember me at the lake.
Remember me on your wedding day,
And save me a piece of cake.

They say it pays to advertise.

There is a pale-blue flower
That twines 'round the shepherd's cot,
And at the midnight hour
It chimes "forget-me-not."

Remember me is all I ask,
But should remembrance be a task,
Forget me.

I will not say, "Forget-me-not."
I know you will not care.
So I'll turn the saying upside down.
Forget me if you dare.

Henry was here and is now gone,
But leaves his name to carry on.

When I am dead and in my grave,
And all my bones are rotten,
This little book will bear my name,
Which long has been forgotten.

Remember me in all your wishes,
Even when you wash the dishes.
If the water gets too hot,
Wring out the rag and forget me not.

Remember the kid from Brooklyn,
Remember the kid from Spain.
Remember the kid from P.S. 10,
And Judy is her name.

If you have a notion
That the ocean
Is full of commotion,
Try the sea
And remember me.

When you are dying
And making your will,
Think of the one
Who wrote uphill.

As years roll by,
As years surely will,
Remember your friend
Who wrote downhill.

When you are drinking
Cold black tea,
Victoria, remember me.
And if by chance
The tea is hot,
Victoria, forget me not.

If you see a monkey in a tree,
Don't throw sticks—it might be me.

In Central Park
There is a rock,
And on it says
"Forget-Me-Not."
Farther down
There is a tree,
And on it's carved,
"Remember Me."

In your woodbox of memories, put in a chip for me.

Remember me
When this you see,
And what a girl
I used to be.

In French there is a little word.
To them it's very dear.
In English it's "forget-me-not,"
In French it's "souvenir."

On this leaf
In memory pressed,
May my name
Forever rest.

If writing in albums
Remembrance assures,
With the greatest of pleasure
I'll write in yours.

Think of a fly,
Think of a flea.
When something tickles you,
Think of me.

Best Wishes, Amen

Can't think,
Brain dumb.
Inspiration won't come.
Poor ink,
Bum pen.
Best wishes,
Amen.

```
┌─────────────────────────────────────────────────┐
│  ┌───────────────────────────────────────────┐  │
│  │                                           │  │
│  │     THE BANK OF SUCCESS                   │  │
│  │   Pay to the order of : Sally Jones       │  │
│  │   The sum of: Health, Wealth              │  │
│  │                and Happiness.             │  │
│  │                                           │  │
│  └───────────────────────────────────────────┘  │
└─────────────────────────────────────────────────┘
```

May your life be a succession of successive successes.

May your luck ever spread
Like jelly on bread.

May your joys be as deep as the ocean
And your sorrows as light as its foam.
May Kansas be your dwelling place
And Heaven your future home.

May your life be strewn with roses
And your children have pug noses.

When the walls of earth have fallen
And this road no more we trod,
May your name in gold be written
In the autograph of God.

Judge—Anne
Court—Public School 6
Prisoner—Connie
Cell—Room 504
Crime—Graduation
Sentence—A life of success and happiness

In the storms of life
When you need an umbrella,
May you have to uphold it
A handsome young fellow.

May your luck be like the capital of Ireland:
"Always Dublin."

May your life be like an old-fashioned gown—
long and beautiful.

May your past be *A Midsummer-Night's Dream*
And your future *As You Like It.*

May you always meet Dame Fortune,
But never her daughter, Miss Fortune.

May your life be long and sunny
And your husband fat and funny.

May your troubles be like the old man's teeth—
few and far apart.

```
W
E
A                    As many fishes as are in the sea,
L                    So many good wishes I wish to thee.
T
H A P P I N E S S
E                 U
A                 C
L                 C
T                 E
H                 S
                  S
```

Sally Smith, M.D.
Office Hours, 9 to 3

Prescription:
    Health
    Wealth
    Happiness
    Success

Shake well and take in large doses

173

Sailing down the stream of life
In your little bark canoe,
May you have a pleasant trip
With just room enough for two.

Long may you live,
Happy may you be,
Blessed with six children,
Three on each knee.

Chicken when you're hungry,
Champagne when you're dry,
A nice man when you're twenty,
And Heaven when you die.

May you always be happy
And live at your ease,
And have a good husband
To tease when you please.

May you gently float
Down the stream of time
Like a bob-tailed rooster
On a watermelon rind.

May your life be like Arithmetic:

Joys **+** (added)
Sorrows **−** (subtracted)
Happiness **✕** (multiplied)
Love Un **÷** (divided)

Take the word "pluck."
Cut off the "p."
What is left
I wish for thee.

I wish you luck,
I wish you joy.
I wish you a bouncing baby boy.
And when his hair
Begins to curl,
I wish you have a baby girl.
And when her hair
Grows straight as pins,
I wish you have a pair of twins.

May your future be as bright
As Broadway at night,
And your heart be as true
As the red, white, and blue.

If you were a fish
And I were a duck,
I'd swim to the bottom
And wish you good luck.

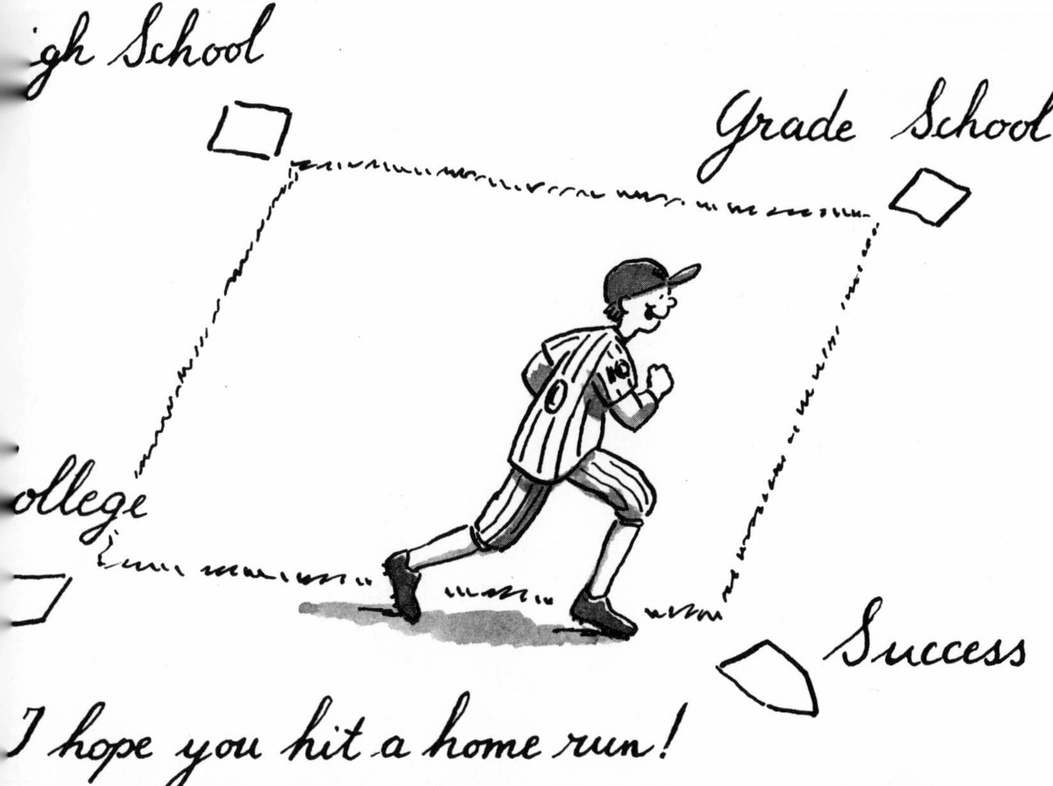

I hope you hit a home run!

Best what?
I forgot.
Oh, of course,
Best wishes.

I wish you health,
Rockefeller's wealth,
Einstein's knowledge,
Through high school and college.

To my friend—
Luck to the end.

ACKNOWLEDGMENT

THESE RHYMES WERE SELECTED from many hundreds found in actual autograph albums. It would be difficult to thank by name all the people who have so kindly lent their albums and supplied me with rhymes over the years—relatives, friends, friends' friends, and scores of boys and girls from the high schools and junior high schools in and around New York. I am especially grateful to the staff of the Aguilar Branch of the New York Public Library and to my co-workers and teenage friends at this library during the period 1943 to 1947. I should also like to thank the English Department of the Central Commercial High School Annex for help in obtaining rhymes, Miss Margaret C. Scoggin of the New York Public Library for encouragement, and Mr. and Mrs. Alvin Samuels for assistance throughout.

—Lillian Morrison
1950